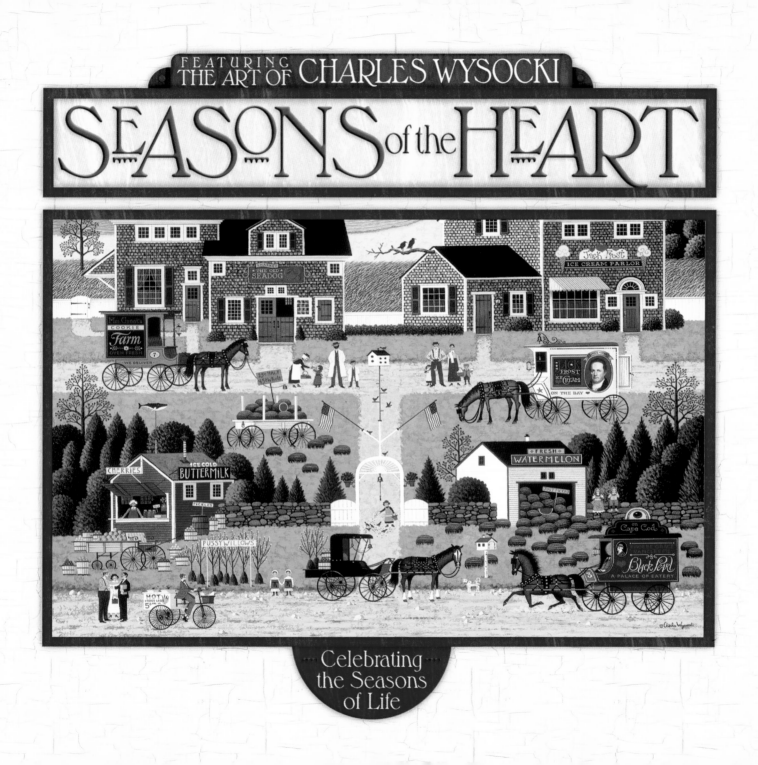

FEATURING
THE ART OF CHARLES WYSOCKI

SEASONS of the HEART

Celebrating
the Seasons
of Life

LIST OF PAINTINGS

CHARLES WYSOCKI, the foremost painter of Early American life today, has brought together his most memorable images for this glorious book.

In a time of utmost sophistication, Chuck beckons us back to a world of honest virtues and charming country landscapes. He revives pleasant thoughts of a bygone era when order, neatness, and serenity ruled, when people were not afraid to show their sentimental affection for home and family, God and country.

Chuck does not just paint beautiful pictures, he touches our heart each and every time by expressing our nostalgic yearnings for a world of remembered joys. The universal appeal of his work has led to many prestigious awards, the reproduction of his art on many successful products and most importantly, to a large and loyal following. As a result, he is one of America's most beloved and respected artists.

Americana® Wall Calendar Artwork

© 1997 AMCAL • © 1997 Charles Wysocki

Text Copyright © 1997 • Brownlow Publishing Company
6309 Airport Freeway, Fort Worth, TX 76117

ISBN 1-57051-200-0

Cover/interior: Koechel Peterson & Associates

Printed in China

SEASONS of the HEART

FEATURING
THE ART OF **CHARLES WYSOCKI** TEXT WRITTEN & COMPILED BY **PAUL C. BROWNLOW**

Brownlow

SEASONS OF THE HEART

According to its God-appointed rhythms, nature renews and repeats itself year after year after year. Spring follows winter as surely as sunrise follows night.

But for us, the physical seasons of our age are to be lived only once. We will only be thirty, forty or fifty once. But if the years are used wisely and lived right, once is enough.

However, there are other seasons, seasons of the heart—those perpetual times of blossoms and harvest that come always. Those seasons, though no less important because they are many, are to be lived and relished daily.

When we are living in the full presence of the moment, fully attuned to the seasons, all of them—the seasons of nature, the season of our years, and most importantly the seasons of our hearts—then life becomes ripe and fruitful, full of flavor and filled with perpetual harvests. Life is resplendent with seasons. Let us rejoice and celebrate those now dawning.

  P.C.B.

THERE IS NO SEASON SUCH DELIGHT CAN BRING
AS SUMMER, AUTUMN, WINTER, AND THE SPRING.

A PRAYER IN SPRING

Oh, give us pleasure in the flowers today;
And give us not to think so far away
As the uncertain harvest; keep us here
All simply in the springing of the year.

Oh, give us pleasure in the orchard white,
Like nothing else by day, like ghosts by night;
And make us happy in the happy bees,
The swarm dilating round the perfect trees.

And make us happy in the darting bird
That suddenly above the bees is heard,
The meteor that thrusts in with needle bill,
And off a blossom in mid air stands still.

For this is love and nothing else is love,
The which it is reserved for God above
To sanctify to what far ends He will,
But which it only needs that we fulfil.

Robert Frost

Spring unlocks the flowers
to paint the laughing soil.

Reginald Heber

If you would reap praise,
sow the seeds;
Gentle words and useful deeds.

Benjamin Franklin

Nothing is so beautiful as spring!

Gerard Manley Hopkins

See! The winter is past;
the rains are over and gone.
Flowers appear on the earth;
the season of singing has come.

Song of Songs 2:11-12

If spring came but once in a
century instead of once a year,
or burst forth with the sound of an
earthquake, and not in silence,
what wonder and expectation there
would be in all hearts to behold the
miraculous change.

Henry Wadsworth Longfellow

There is no time like spring
When life's alive in everything.

Christina Georgina Rossetti

The world is not painted or
adorned, but is from the beginning
beautiful.

Ralph Waldo Emerson

THE REDISCOVERY OF LIFE

We are once again rediscovering the hollowness of life that feeds itself on husks and externals, and then wonders why there is an emptiness within our hearts. Though a dazzling new array of technological toys promise excitement and fulfillment, the meaning of life has been lost in the haste to acquire these trinkets.

It is with sad amusement that we read again Henry David Thoreau's assessment more than a hundred and fifty years ago regarding the hurry and waste of life. Those were the days we now dream of. How could he be so hurried? But in the end, he bluntly concludes, "The world lives too fast." So it is in our own day that a bushel of new books and new authors decry the same hurry and haste and prescribe the same remedies.

Once again we attempt the journey back to the simple elements long abandoned and seek our joys in small pleasures, longing to live quiet lives of contentment.

And, weary seekers of the best,
We come back laden from our quest
To find that all the sages said
Is in the Book our mothers read.

JOHN GREENLEAF WHITTIER

God grants these joys and contentments only when we fully inhale and absorb the air around us—our families, our homes, our children, our friends. We rediscover life when we serve our God by humbly serving and loving His children. We recapture meaning when we learn that happiness grows at our own firesides, and not in other people's gardens. Finally the frantic doing and having must give way to being. The world will always live too fast. But we are not the world. We are each a single soul, and we choose not only the path of life but the pace.

P.C.B.

SEASONS of JOY

Joy of life seems to me to arise from a sense of being where one belongs. All the discontented people I know are trying to be something they are not, to do something they cannot do. Contentment, and indeed usefulness, comes as the infallible result of great acceptances, great humilities—of not trying to make ourselves this or that (to conform to some dramatized version of ourselves), but of surrendering ourselves to the fullness of life—of letting life flow through us.

☙ DAVID GRAYSON

Joy is never in our power, and pleasure is. I doubt whether anyone who has tasted joy would ever, if both were in his power, exchange it for all the pleasure in the world.

☙ C. S. LEWIS

Fill me with joy in your presence.

☙ PSALM 16:11

Joy can be real only if people look upon their life as a service, and have a definite object in life outside themselves and their personal happiness.

☙ LEO TOLSTOY

It is a poor heart that never rejoices.

☙ EARLY AMERICAN PROVERB

Joy is a positive thing: in joy one does not only feel secure, but something goes out from oneself to the universe, a warm, positive effluence of love.

☙ RICHARD HOOKER

True joy is not a thing of moods, not a capricious emotion, tied to fluctuating experiences. It is a state and condition of the soul. It survives through pain and sorrow and, like a subterranean spring, waters the whole life. It is intimately allied and bound up with love and goodness, and so is deeply rooted in the life of God.

☙ RUFUS MATTHEW JONES

The word joy is too great and grand to be confused with the superficial things we call happiness.

☙ KIRBY PAGE

There is no beautifier of complexion, or form, or behavior, like the wish to scatter joy and not pain around us.

☙ SAMUEL TAYLOR COLERIDGE

Life's a patchwork quilt made from bits and pieces of joy and sadness, sewn together with love.

☙ ANONYMOUS

The joy that you give to others
Is the joy that comes back to you.

☙ JOHN GREENLEAF WHITTIER

Joy is not in things,
it is in us.

RICHARD WAGNER

A PLACE FOR JOY

Take joy home,
and make a place in thy great
heart for her,
and give her time to grow,
and cherish her!
Then will she come
and often sing to thee
when thou art working
in the furrows; ay,
or weeding in the
sacred hour of dawn.
It is a comely fashion
to be glad.
Joy is the grace
we say to God.

Jean Ingelow

SEASONS OF HAPPINESS

Happiness is the greatest paradox in Nature. It can grow in any soil, live under any conditions. It defies environment. It comes from within; it reveals the depths of the inner life as light and heat proclaim the sun from which they radiate. Happiness consists not of having, but of being; not of possessing, but of enjoying. It is the warm glow of a heart at peace with itself.

Happiness represents a peaceful attunement of a life with a goal. It can never be made by the individual, by himself, for himself. It is one of the incidental by-products of an unselfish life. No one can make his own happiness the one object of his life and attain it, any more than he can jump on the far end of his shadow. If you would hit the bull's-eye of happiness on the target of life, aim above it. Place other things higher than your own happiness and it will surely come to you. You can buy pleasure, you can acquire contentment, you can become satisfied, but God never put real happiness on the bargain counter. It is the undetachable accompaniment of true living. It is calm and peaceful; it never lives in an atmosphere of worry or of hopeless struggle.

The basis of happiness is the love of something outside self. Search every instance of happiness in the world, and you will find, when all the incidental features are eliminated, there is always the constant, unchangeable element of love: love of parent for child; love of man and woman for each other; love of humanity in some form, or a great life work into which the individual throws all his energies.

Unhappiness is the hunger to get; happiness is the hunger to give. True happiness must ever have the tinge of sorrow outlived, the sense of pain softened by the mellowing years, the chastening of loss that in the wondrous mystery of time transmutes our suffering into love and sympathy with others.

If the individual should set out for a single day to give happiness, to make life happier, brighter and sweeter, not for himself, but for others, he would find a wondrous revelation of what happiness really is. The greatest of the world's heroes could not by any series of acts of heroism do as much real good as any individual living his whole life in seeking, from day to day, to make others happy.

& WILLIAM GEORGE JORDAN, *Former Editor of the Saturday Evening Post*

Those who dwell among the beauties and mysteries of the earth are never alone or weary of life.

RACHEL CARSON

Charles Wysocki

ABOVE THE WORLD

THE WORLD STANDS OUT
ON EITHER SIDE
NO WIDER THAN THE
HEART IS WIDE;
ABOVE THE WORLD IS
STRETCHED THE SKY—
NO HIGHER THAN THE
SOUL IS HIGH.
THE HEART CAN PUSH
THE SEA AND LAND
FARTHER AWAY ON
EITHER HAND;
THE SOUL CAN SPLIT
THE SKY IN TWO,
AND LET THE FACE OF
GOD SHINE THROUGH.

EDNA ST. VINCENT MILLAY

The human heart is large enough to contain any amount of happiness.
& T. W. ROBERTSON

We can only have the highest happiness by having wide thoughts, and much feeling for the rest of the world, as well as ourselves.
& GEORGE ELIOT

Blessed are they who are pleasant to live with.
& ANONYMOUS

Make happy those who are near, and those who are far will come.
& PROVERB

Most folks are about as happy as they make up their minds to be.
& ABRAHAM LINCOLN

To live in the happy sufficing present: to find the day and its chief means contenting: to fill the hour—that is Happiness.
& RALPH WALDO EMERSON

A cheerful look brings joy to the heart, and good news gives health to the bones. A cheerful heart is good medicine, but a crushed spirit dries up the bones.
& PROVERBS 15:30; 17:22

A small house will hold as much happiness as a big one.
& EARLY AMERICAN PROVERB

I have learned from experience that the greater part of our happiness or misery depends on our dispositions and not on our circumstances.
& MARTHA WASHINGTON

Do whatever comes your way to do as well as you can. Think as little as possible about yourself and as much as possible about other people and about things that are interesting. Put a good deal of thought into happiness that you are able to give.
& ELEANOR ROOSEVELT

A New England Summer

Whoe'er thou art,
who walkest there
Where God first taught my feet to roam,
Breathe but my name into the air,
I am content, for that is home.

A sense, a color comes to me,
Of baybushes that heavy lie
With juniper along the sea,
And the blue sea along the sky.

New England my home; 'tis there
I love the rising Sun and Moon.
'Tis there I love the growing year,
December and young-summer June.

&ð PHILIP HENRY SAVAGE

I expect some new phases of life this summer, and shall try to get the honey from each moment.
&ð LUCY STONE

Antiques restore our sense of balance, our sense of the familiar as we run headlong into the unknown future. Antiques not only add grace to our homes, they restore calm to our souls.
&ð ANONYMOUS

Not only the days, but life itself lengthens in summer. I would spread abroad my arms and gather more of it to me, could I do so.
&ð RICHARD JEFFERIES

We blossom under praise like flowers in sun and dew; we open, we reach, we grow.
GERHARD E. FROST

I will be the gladdest thing under the sun, I will touch a hundred flowers and not pick one.
&ð EDNA ST. VINCENT MILLAY

When you buy the land, you buy the stones; when you buy the meat, you buy the bones.
&ð VERMONT PROVERB

He has made everything beautiful in its time.
&ð ECCLESIASTES 3:11

There is nothing that makes men rich and strong but that which they carry inside of them. Wealth is of the heart, not of the hand.
&ð JOHN MILTON

Touch the earth, love the earth, honor the earth, her plains, her valleys, her hills, and her seas; rest your spirit in her solitary places.
&ð HENRY BESTON

God doesn't have to put His name on a label in the corner of a meadow because nobody else makes meadows.
&ð CECIL LAIRD

SEASONS OF LOVE

Love is the one ingredient of which our world never tires and of which there is never an abundance. It is needed in the marketplace and in the mansions. It is needed in the ghettos and in the governments. It is needed in homes, in hospitals, and in individual hearts. The world will never outgrow its need for love.

        C. NEIL STRAIT

Love cannot be forced, love cannot be coaxed and teased. It comes out of Heaven, unasked and unsought.

 PEARL BUCK

If you have love in your heart, you will always have something to give.

 ANONYMOUS

We must strengthen, defend, preserve and comfort each other. We must love one another.

 JOHN WINTHROP
Founder, Massachusetts Bay Colony

I love you for what you are, but I love you yet more for what you are going to be. I love you not so much for your realities as for your ideals. I pray for your desires that they may be great, rather than for your satisfactions, which may be so hazardously little. You are going forward toward something great. I am on the way with you, and therefore I love you.

 CARL SANDBURG

Let love and faithfulness never leave you.

 PROVERBS 3:3

The cure for all the ills and wrongs, the cares, the sorrows, and the crimes of humanity, all lie in the one word "love." It is the divine vitality that everywhere produces and restores life.

 LYDIA MARIA CHILD

We never live so intensely as when we love strongly. We never realize ourselves so vividly as when we are in the full glow of love for others.

 WALTER RAUSCHENBUSCH

Blessed is he that truly loves and seeketh not love in return.

 FRANCIS OF ASSISI

No burden is heavy when it is carried with love.

 EARLY AMERICAN PROVERB

EARLY AMERICAN FOLK WISDOM

It is better to deserve without receiving than to receive without deserving.

Each year, one vicious habit rooted out in time ought to make the worst man good.

She is but half a wife who is not a friend.

The early morning has gold in its mouth.

If a man empties his purse into his head, no man can take it away from him. An investment in knowledge always pays the best interest.

He that is good for making excuses is seldom good for anything else.

Experience keeps a dear school, but fools will learn in no other.

A homemade friend wears longer than one you buy in the market.

Wisdom is to the soul what health is to the body.

Thought is the blossom; language the bud; action the fruit behind it.

Age does not endow all old things with strength and virtue, nor are all new things to be despised.

Men, like peaches and pears, grow sweet a little while before they begin to decay.

We are born believing. A man bears beliefs, as a tree bears apples.

Little boats should keep near shore.

A child's education should begin at least one hundred years before he is born.

A torn jacket is soon mended, but harsh words bruise the heart of a child.

Life is not so short but that there is always time for courtesy.

If you would sleep soundly, take a clear conscience to bed with you.

Let thy child's first lesson be obedience, and the second will be what thou wilt.

Heaven does not make holiness, but holiness makes heaven.

There never was any heart
truly great and generous,
that was not also
tender and compassionate.

ROBERT FROST

I took a day to search for God,
And found Him not. But as I trod
By rocky ledge, through woods untamed,
I saw His footprint in the sod.

Then suddenly, all unaware,
Far off in the deep shadows, where
A solitary hermit thrush
Sang through the holy twilight hush—
I heard His voice upon the air.

And even as I marvelled how
God gives us Heaven here and now,
In a stir of wind that hardly shook
The poplar leaves beside the brook—
His hand was light upon my brow.

At last with evening as I turned
Homeward, and thought what I had learned
And all that there was still to probe—
I caught the glory of His robe
Where the last fires of sunset burned.

Back to the world with quickening start
I looked and longed for any part
In making saving Beauty be.
And from that kindling ecstasy
I knew God dwelt within my heart.

BLISS CARMAN

SEASONS of FRIENDSHIP

There can be no friendship where there is no freedom. Friendship loves a free air, and will not be penned up in straight and narrow enclosures. It will speak freely, and act so too; and take nothing ill where no ill is meant; nay, where it is, 'twill easily forgive, and forget too, upon small acknowledgments. Friends are true twins in soul; they sympathise in everything.

One is not happy without the other, nor can either of them be miserable alone. As if they could change bodies, they take their turns in pain as well as in pleasure; relieving one another in their most adverse conditions.

  WILLIAM PENN
    Founder, The Pennsylvania Colony

Unlike most men, Ralph Waldo Emerson knew the inestimable value of friendship. After years of careful observation, he left these thoughts to share with the world. Here are but a few of his conclusions:

Our chief want in life is somebody who shall make us do what we can. This is the service of a friend. With him we are easily great. There is a sublime attraction in him to whatever virtue there is in us. How he flings wide open the door of existence! What questions we ask of him! What an understanding we have. How few words are needed!

Remember—we must be our own before we can be another's. There must be two before there can be one.

God evidently does not intend us all to be rich, or powerful, or great, but He does intend us all to be friends.

I awoke this morning with devout thanksgiving for my friends, the old and the new. I am not so ungrateful as not to see the wise, the lovely and the noble-minded as from time to time they pass my gate.

All are needed by
  each one;
Nothing is fair or good
  alone.

SAFE HARBOR

A friend is a safe harbor. In her presence, the winds and waves of our turbulent lives are stilled, and we are at rest.

It is a peaceful calm where the great cargoes of life—family joys, simple pleasures, the tokens of friendship—can be transferred from one another, from ship to harbor and back again.

While ships were not made to stay in harbor, the time of harbor is a necessity. Neither ships nor persons can stay at sea forever; they must periodically seek harbor or perish. There they are fitted and prepared with fresh supplies for the coming journey. So it is with a friend.

In harbor, we are renewed. In harbor, we are at rest. In harbor, we are blessed.

&& P.C.B.

Once in an age, God sends to some of us a friend who loves in us…not the person that we are, but the angel we may be.

&& HARRIET BEECHER STOWE

There can be no unity, no delight of love, no harmony, no good in being, where there is but one. Two at least are needed for oneness.

&& GEORGE MACDONALD

There are three things that grow more precious with age: old wood to burn, old books to read, and old friends to enjoy.

&& EARLY AMERICAN PROVERB

Give what you have. To someone it may be better than you dare to think.

&& HENRY WADSWORTH LONGFELLOW

Be courteous to all, but intimate with few, and let those few be well tried before you give them your confidence. True friendship is a plant of slow growth and must undergo and withstand the shocks of adversity.

&& GEORGE WASHINGTON

The greatest service one can perform is to be a friend to someone. Friendship is not only doing something for someone, but it is caring for someone, which is what every person needs.

&& C. NEIL STRAIT

No one can develop fully in this world and find a full life without feeling understood by at least one person.

&& PAUL TOURNIER

AS FOR WHAT YOU'RE CALLING HARD LUCK—WELL, WE MADE NEW ENGLAND OUT OF IT, THAT AND CODFISH.

STEPHEN VINCENT BENÉT

I still find each day too short for all the thoughts I want to think, all the walks I want to take, all the books I want to read, and all the friends I want to see. The longer I live, the more my mind dwells upon the beauty and wonder of the world.

⚓ JOHN BURROUGHS

True friends have no solitary joy or sorrow.

⚓ WILLIAM ELLERY CHANNING

Nobody has ever measured, not even poets, how much the heart can hold.

⚓ ZELDA FITZGERALD

Better one true friend than a hundred acquaintances.

⚓ EARLY AMERICAN PROVERB

Do good to your friend to keep him, to your enemy to gain him.

⚓ BENJAMIN FRANKLIN

Those who love deeply never grow old; they may die of old age, but they die young.

⚓ SIR ARTHUR WING PINERO

Old quilts, old times, old manners, old friends.

⚓ EARLY AMERICAN MOTTO

Like cuttlefish we conceal ourselves, we darken the atmosphere in which we move; we are not transparent. I pine for one to whom I can speak my first thoughts; thoughts which represent me truly, which are no better and no worse than I; thoughts which have the bloom on them, which alone can be sacred or divine.

⚓ HENRY DAVID THOREAU

He who has friends must be friendly.

⚓ PROVERBS 18:24

Life is made up, not of great sacrifices or duties, but of little things, in which smiles, and kindnesses, and small obligations, given habitually, are what win and preserve the heart and secure comfort.

⚓ SIR HUMPHREY DAVY

AUTUMN DAYS

Autumn days turn our hearts toward harvest. Harvest time—the reaping of what has been planted, worked, trimmed and patiently waited for. It is the reward, the fruition of our efforts.

Be it corn or character, the principle is the same. The farmer doesn't wait till autumn to decide what kind of harvest he wants. He plans, prepares and pursues the crop long months before. Silently and alone, in front of a winter fireplace, the farmer studies the seed catalog and sees the harvest as clearly as if it were real.

We plant today the harvest of tomorrow. The seeds of life are all around us. We must only choose our crops and begin.

& P.C.B.

The earth's distances invite the eye. And as the eye reaches, so must the mind stretch to meet these new horizons. I challenge anyone to stand with autumn on a hilltop and fail to see a new expanse, not only around him, but in him, too.

& HAL BORLAND

When so rich a harvest is before us, why do we not gather it? All is in our hands if we will but use it.

& ELIZABETH SETON

Man, unlike nature, can have spring times in autumn.

& PAUL TOURNIER

There are still, in October, a few red apples on the boughs of the trees in a little orchard beside the road.

& RICHARD JEFFERIES

Good thoughts bear good fruit, bad thoughts bear bad fruit—and man is his own gardener.

& JAMES ALLEN

For the Lord your God will bless you in all your harvest and in all the work of your hands, and your joy will be complete.

& DEUTERONOMY 16:15

Hands to work, Hearts to God.

& EARLY SHAKER MOTTO

THE FARMERS ALMANAC
of 1794

❧A contented mind and a good conscience will make a man happy in all conditions.

❧Prosperity gains friends, and adversity tries them.

❧Complaisance renders a superior amiable, an equal agreeable, and an inferior acceptable.

❧By the faults of others wise men correct their own.

❧Pitch upon that course of life which is most pleasant, and custom will render it the most delightful.

❧Without a friend the world is but a wilderness.

❧Anger may glance into the breast of a wise man, but rests only in the bosom of a fool.

❧He who is truly polite knows how to contradict with respect and to please without adulation— and is equally remote from insipid complaisance and low familiarity.

❧Honor thy father with thy whole heart, and forget not the sorrows of thy mother: how canst thou recompense them for the things they have done for thee?

❧Truth is always consistent with itself and needs nothing to help it out, whereas a lie is troublesome and sets a man's invention on the rack—and one trick needs a great many more to make it good.

❧Many men have been capable of doing a wise thing—more, a cunning thing—but very few, a generous thing.

FOR POTTAGE AND
PUDDINGS AND
CUSTARDS AND PIES,
OUR PUMPKINS
AND PARSNIPS ARE
COMMON SUPPLIES,
WE HAVE PUMPKINS
AT MORNING AND
PUMPKINS AT NOON,
IF IT WERE NOT FOR
PUMPKINS WE SHOULD
BE UNDOON.

PILGRIM VERSE, CIRCA 1630

SEASONS OF PEACE

ONLY IN

QUIET WATERS

THINGS MIRROR

THEMSELVES

UNDISTORTED.

ONLY IN A

QUIET MIND

IS ADEQUATE

PERCEPTION OF

THE WORLD.

HANS MARGOLIUS

But real action is in silent moments. The epochs of our life are not in the visible facts of our choice of a calling, our marriage, our acquisition of an office, and the like, but in a silent thought by the wayside as we walk.

& RALPH WALDO EMERSON

There will be peace in the world so far as there is righteousness in the heart.

& JOHN MILLER

The world is full of untold novelties for him who has the eyes to see them.

& THOMAS HUXLEY

Be still and strong, and keep thy soul's large window pure from wrong.

& ELIZABETH BARRETT BROWNING

Peace cannot be kept by force. It can only be achieved by understanding.

& ALBERT EINSTEIN

Better an egg in peace than an ox in war.

& EARLY AMERICAN PROVERB

I would set out by myself before the family was stirring in the morning and spend whole days in the woods, which required of me only that I be silent, patient and harmless. In return, nature gave me the peace that it gives to any-one who comes to see and hear and not to change.

& W. CHAMBERS

True peace is found by man in the depths of his own heart, the dwelling place of God.

& JOHANN TAULER

Salute the day with peaceful thoughts, And peace will fill your heart; Begin the day with joyful soul, And joy will be your part.

& FRANK B. WHITNEY

Peacemakers who sow in peace raise a harvest of righteousness.

& JAMES 3:18

EVERY DAY IS SACRED

Every morning God quietly and routinely pours another twenty-four hours of existence into our small cupped hands. We, so dazed and benumbed by its everlasting regularity, are careless—letting slip some of the precious moments He has given. Most often, we take the day for granted without realizing it was never promised, never put into a contract, never guaranteed.

But must we continue ignoring our blessings because they be so abundant? We can choose to live life as a sacred gift, but to do so we must live with intentionality and purpose. We must remember that peace of mind is from within and has nothing to do with surface surroundings. We must remember the philosopher's words that "living requires practice, like playing the violin," and that we will get better at living life as we go on. We must remember that life is really found between the two great everlasting eternities of Yesterday and Tomorrow. While both are important, we must be slaves to neither. It is the Present Moment, the Divine Today that we serve, and that in turn serves us. We must daily seek out kindred spirits, those dear souls who share and relish our need to discover all the sweet richness each day brings.

When every day is sacred, we will find contentment in the midst of turmoil, depth in the pools of shallowness, quietness among the clamor of the crowd. Life will then be truly a gift from God—a gift we receive with expectancy and treasure with gratitude.

& P.C.B.

Though we travel the world over to find the beautiful, we must carry it with us or we find it not.
& RALPH WALDO EMERSON

There is no part of America where the people and the soil fit as they seem to do in Pennsylvania.
& WALLACE NUTTING

He is happiest, be he king or peasant, who finds peace in his home.
& JOHANN WOLFGANG VON GOETHE

Lord of the far
    horizons,
Give us the eyes to see
Over the verge of the
    sundown
The beauty that is to be.
& BLISS CARMAN

A THANKFUL SPIRIT

First among the things to be thankful for is a thankful spirit. Some people would grumble at the accommodations in Heaven if they ever got there. They take their blessings here so much as a matter of course, that even a day of general thanksgiving once a year is more than they feel any need of. And if their personal blessings in any measure fail, gratitude for what they have had or still enjoy is the last thing they think of. Another group really desire to be thankful, but they are naturally despondent. Their sky is dark with clouds as they go through the world in a deprecating spirit, hoping things may turn out well yet fearing for the worst. We always feel glad for this group when Thanksgiving Day comes around. They then have an official reason for gratitude. If their own hearts do not feel blessings, perhaps they can see it in those around them.

How different with the thankful heart! What a gift it is to be born with an outlook toward the bright side of things! And if not so by nature, what a triumph of grace to be made thankful through a renewed heart! It is so much more comfortable and rational to see what we have to be thankful for and to rejoice accordingly, than to have our vision for ever filled with our lacks and our needs. Happy are they who possess this gift! Blessings may fail and fortunes vary, but the thankful heart remains. The happy past is secure—and Heaven is ahead.

AND LET US GIVE THANKS FOR SOMEONE TO THANK. GERHARD E. FROST

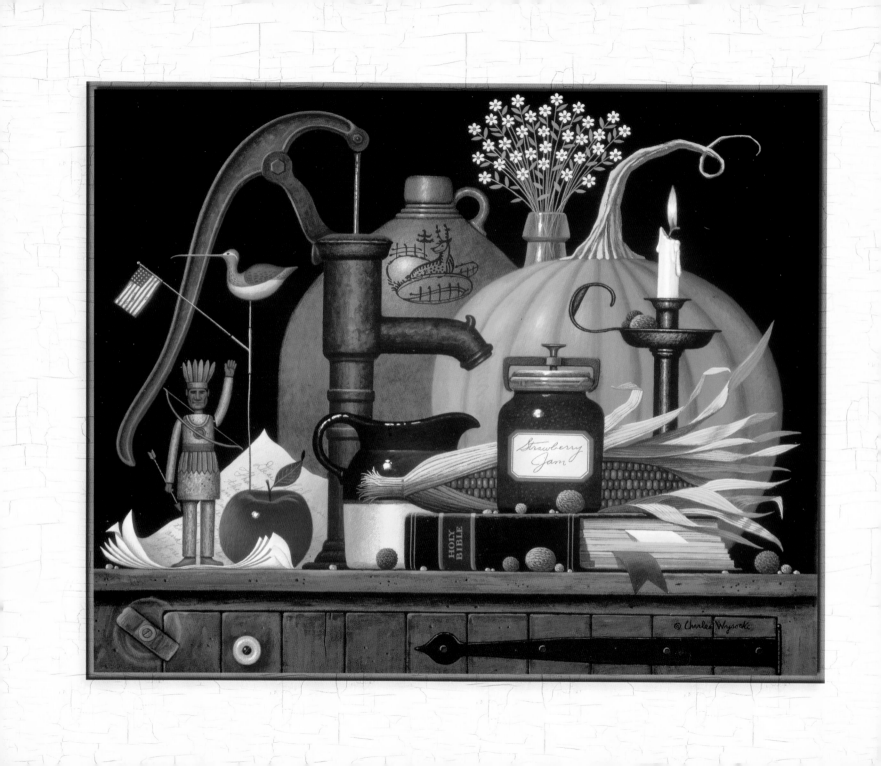

THANKSGIVING DAY, 1789

Whereas it is the duty of all nations to acknowledge the providence of Almighty God, to obey His will, to be grateful for His benefits, and humbly to implore His protection and favor.

Now, therefore, I do recommend and assign Thursday, the twenty-sixth day of November next, to be devoted by the people of these United States that we then may all unite unto Him our sincere and humble thanks for His kind care and protection of the people of this country previous to their becoming a nation; for the signal and manifold mercies and the favorable interpositions of His providence in the course and conclusion of the late war.

❧ PRESIDENT GEORGE WASHINGTON

So it is, life is actually made up of our choices. We are the sum total of them, and if we hold to an attitude of love and thanksgiving for all the good things within our grasp we may have what all ambitious people long for—success.

❧ DELMA NEELEY

Cultivate the thankful spirit! It will be to you a perpetual feast.

❧ JOHN R. MACDUFF

Were there no God we would be in this glorious world with grateful hearts and no one to thank.

❧ CHRISTINA GEORGINA ROSSETTI

Who does not thank for little will not thank for much.

❧ EARLY AMERICAN PROVERB

Give thanks to the Lord, for he is good. His love endures forever.

❧ PSALM 136:1

Remember the day's blessings; forget the day's troubles.

❧ EARLY AMERICAN PROVERB

Life without thankfulness is devoid of love and passion. Hope without thankfulness is lacking in fine perception. Faith without thankfulness lacks strength and fortitude. Every virtue divorced from thankfulness is maimed and limps along the spiritual road.

❧ JOHN HENRY JOWETT

Not what we say about our blessings but how we use them is the true measure of our thanksgiving

❧ W. T. PURKISER

LET THE HEAVENS REJOICE, LET THE EARTH BE GLAD; LET THE SEA RESOUND, AND ALL THAT IS IN IT; LET THE FIELDS BE JUBILANT, AND EVERYTHING IN THEM. THEN ALL THE TREES OF THE FOREST WILL SING FOR JOY; THEY WILL SING BEFORE THE LORD.

PSALM 96: 11-13

The holiest of all holidays are those kept by ourselves in silence and apart: the secret anniversaries of the heart.

& HENRY WADSWORTH LONGFELLOW

If you would enter deeply into the meaning of thanksgiving, cultivate the mood of expectant love, the attitude of awe before the marvelous, and the openheartedness that turns in confidence to that source from whence we sprung.

& HENRY DAVID GRAY

Gratitude is the memory of the heart.

& MASSIEU

It is only with gratitude that life becomes rich.

& DIETRICH BONHOEFFER

It is a sad thing to reflect that in a world so overflowing with goodness of smell, of fine sights and sweet sounds, we pass by hastily and take so little note of them.

& DAVID GRAYSON

The Pilgrims made seven times more graves than huts. No Americans have been more impoverished than those—who, nevertheless, set aside a day of thanksgiving.

& W. A. WESTERMEYER

Pride slays thanksgiving, but a humble mind is the soil out of which thanks naturally grows. A proud man is seldom a grateful man; he never thinks he gets as much as he deserves.

& HENRY WARD BEECHER

When it comes to life, the critical thing is whether you take things for granted or take them with gratitude.

& G. K. CHESTERTON

God has two dwellings: one in heaven, and the other in a meek and thankful heart.

& IZAAK WALTON

The sunshine smiles upon the winter days of my heart, never doubting of its spring flowers.

RABINDRANATH TAGORE

A CELEBRATION
OF WINTER

The inhabitants of cities suppose

that the country landscape

is pleasant only half the year.

I please myself with the graces

of the winter scenery, and believe

that we are as much touched by it

as by the genial influences of

summer. To the attentive eye,

each moment of the year has its

own beauty, and in the same field

it beholds, every hour, a picture

which was never seen before, and

which shall never be seen again.

RALPH WALDO EMERSON

SEASONS OF FAITH

We cannot tell what may happen to us in the strange medley of life. But we can decide what happens in us—how we can take it, what we do with it—and that is what really counts in the end. How to take the raw stuff of life and make it a thing of worth and beauty—that is the test of living. Life is an adventure of faith if we are to be victors over it, not victims of it.

& ANONYMOUS

There is no great future for any people whose faith has burned out.
& RUFUS M. JONES

It is only by forgetting yourself that you draw near to God.
& HENRY DAVID THOREAU

Work as if you were to live a hundred years; pray as if you were to die tomorrow.
& BENJAMIN FRANKLIN

The only limit to our realization of tomorrow will be our doubts of today. Let us move forward with strong and active faith.
& FRANKLIN D. ROOSEVELT

It's faith in something and enthusiasm for something that makes life worth looking at.
& OLIVER WENDELL HOLMES

You can do very little with faith, but you can do nothing without it.
& NICHOLAS MURRAY BUTLER

True faith is never found alone; it is accompanied by expectation.
& C. S. LEWIS

When faith is lost, when honor dies, the man is dead.
& JOHN GREENLEAF WHITTIER

I can see how it might be possible for a man to look down upon the earth and be an atheist, but I cannot conceive how he could look up into the heavens and say there is no God.
& ABRAHAM LINCOLN

I do not want merely to possess a faith; I want a faith that possesses me.
& CHARLES KINGSLEY

Real faith is not the stuff dreams are made of; rather it is tough, practical and altogether realistic. Faith sees the invisible but it does not see the nonexistent.
& A.W. TOZER

STOPPING BY WOODS ON A SNOWY EVENING

Whose woods these are
I think I know.
His house is in the village, though;
He will not see me stopping here
To watch his woods fill up with snow.

My little horse must think it queer
To stop without a farmhouse near
Between the woods and frozen lake
The darkest evening of the year.

He gives his harness bells a shake
To ask if there is some mistake.
The only other sound's the sweep
Of easy wind and downy flake.

The woods are lovely, dark and deep,
But I have promises to keep,
And miles to go before I sleep,
And miles to go before I sleep.

  ROBERT FROST

Love wakes anew
  this throbbing heart,
And we are never old.
Over the winter glaciers
I see the summer glow,
And through the wild-piled
  snowdrift,
The warm rosebuds glow.

  RALPH WALDO EMERSON

God gives us memory
so that we may have roses
in December.

  SIR JAMES BARRIE

If winter comes, can
spring be far behind?

  PERCY BYSSHE SHELLEY

There is not enough
darkness in all the world
to put out the light of one
small candle.

  ANONYMOUS

Be glad of life because
it gives you the chance to
love and to work and to
play and to look at the stars.

  HENRY VAN DYKE

Having some place
to go is home. Having
someone to love is family.
Having both is a blessing.

  ANONYMOUS

A dear old Quaker
lady, distinguished for her
youthful appearance, was
asked what she used to
preserve her appearance.
She replied sweetly, "I use
for the lips, truth; for the
voice, prayer; for the eyes,
pity; for the hand, charity;
for the figure, uprightness;
and for the heart, love."

  JERRY FLEISHMAN

By day the Lord
directs his love, at night
his song is with me.

  PSALM 42:8

LIVING IN HOPE

Everything that is done in the world is done in hope. No farmer would sow one grain of corn if he hoped not it would grow, feed his family, and become more seed; no merchant or trades-man would set himself up to work if he did not hope to reap a benefit thereby; no man and woman would marry if they hoped not for children and pleasant years together. Everything that is done is done in hope—it is the passion that animates activity and gives life to living.

& MARTIN LUTHER

To be seventy years young is sometimes far more cheerful and hopeful than to be forty years old.

& OLIVER WENDELL HOLMES

I live on hope and that I think do all Who come into this world.

& ROBERT BRIDGES

It is impossible for that man to despair who remembers that his Helper is omnipotent.

& JEREMY TAYLOR

Hope is a vigorous principle; it sets the head and heart to work and animates a man to do his utmost.

& JEREMY COLLIER

Hope is like the sun, which, as we journey toward it, casts the shadow of our burden behind us.

S. SMILES

Hope deferred makes the heart sick; but when dreams come true at last, there is life and joy.

& PROVERBS 13:12

There is no medicine like hope, no incentive so great, and no tonic so powerful as expectation of something tomorrow.

& O. S. MARDEN

Of all the forces that make for a better world, none is so indispensable, none so powerful, as hope. Without hope men are only half alive.

& CHARLES SAWYER

The word which God has written on the brow of every man is Hope.

VICTOR HUGO

Hope is the thing with feathers, that perches in the soul, and sings the tune without the words, and never stops at all.

EMILY DICKINSON

You cannot put a great hope into a small soul.

& JENKIN LLOYD-JONES

He who lives in hope dances without a fiddle.

& EARLY AMERICAN PROVERB

Hope arouses, as nothing else can arouse, a passion for the possible.

& WILLIAM SLOANE COFFIN, JR.

BELLS OF CHRISTMAS

Why do the bells
of Christmas ring?
Why do little children sing?

Once a lovely, shining star,
Seen by shepherds from afar,
Gently moved until its light
Made a manger's cradle bright.

There a darling baby lay,
Pillowed soft upon the hay;
And its mother sung
and smiled,
"This is Christ, the holy child!"

Therefore bells for
Christmas ring,
Therefore little children sing.

EUGENE FIELD

Think of me with love
I pray
Upon this Happy
Christmas day.

19TH-CENTURY CHRISTMAS CARD

Christmas began in the
heart of God. It is complete
only when it reaches the
heart of man.

Everywhere, everywhere,
Christmas tonight!
Christmas in lands
    of the palm tree and vine;
Christmas where snow-peaks
    stand solemn and white,
Christmas where cornfields
    lie sunny and bright.

PHILLIPS BROOKS

The joy of brightening
other lives, bearing each
others' burdens, easing
others' loads and supplant-
ing empty hearts and lives
with generous gifts
becomes for us the magic
of Christmas.

W. C. JONES

The only really blind
person at Christmastime is
he who has not Christmas
in his heart.

HELEN KELLER

O Christmas!
Merry Christmas!
Is it really come again?

May joy come from
heaven above
To all those who Christmas
love.

19TH-CENTURY CHRISTMAS CARD

It is Christmas in the
heart that puts Christmas
in the air.

ANONYMOUS

From our snug fireside
this Christmas-tide
We'll keep old Winter out.

THOMAS NOEL

The finest Christmas
gift is not the one that
costs the most money, but
the one that carries the
most love.

HENRY VAN DYKE

OUR SNOW MAN, OUR SNOW MAN,
WE'VE BUILT HIM UP IN HASTE;
WE KNEW NOT WHEN
THE FROST MIGHT BREAK,
WE HAD NO TIME TO WASTE;
SO FIRST WE GATHERED
UP THE SNOW, AND
PILED IT IN A HEAP;
FOR MELONS, ICE,
AND SNOW MEN,
ARE THINGS
THAT WILL
NOT KEEP.

Charles Wysocki

CHRISTMAS IN OUR HEART

It is Christmas
in the mansion,
Yule-log fires
and silken frocks;
It is Christmas
in the cottage,
Mother's filling
little socks.

It is Christmas
on the highway,
In the thronging,
busy mart;
But the dearest
truest Christmas
Is the Christmas
in the heart.

AUTHOR UNKNOWN

© Charles Wysocki

It is good to be children sometimes, and never better than at Christmas, when its mighty Founder was a child himself.

— CHARLES DICKENS

The name of Louis Prang stands out in the relatively short history of American Christmas cards. Prang, a German exile following their revolution of 1848, came to America and introduced art to public schools. In 1874 in Roxbury, Massachusetts, he began printing cards by perfecting a lithographic process employing up to 20 colors. Designs for these Christmas cards were acquired through contests which offered cash prizes to artists throughout America.

Let everything that has breath praise the Lord.

— PSALM 150:6

Christmas is the delight of loving and being loved in return, not for gifts tied with bows but for gifts of the spirit offered with an open heart every day of the year.

— PEARL BUCK

The holidays we set aside and celebrate, no matter what our creed, are part of us always; marked on a calendar, but more deeply etched upon the spirit. But the true rejoicing, the going forward to promises in which you believe, are not really ruled by calendars. Thay are in the heart and pulse and soul.

— FAITH BALDWIN

And so, at this Christmas time, I greet you. Not quite as the world sends greetings, but with profound esteem and with the prayer that for you, now and forever, the day breaks and the shadows flee away.

— FRA GIOVANNI

I like to take my Christmas a little at a time, all through the year. And thus I drift along into the holidays waking up some fine morning and suddenly saying to myself: "Why, this is Christmas Day!"

— DAVID GRAYSON

The very first Christmas celebration in America, according to the records we have, predated the arrival of the Pilgrims. It occurred in 1607 in Jamestown, Virginia, where 40 survivors of the 100 original settlers tried to raise their somber, uncertain spirits by saluting the birth of Christ in their small chapel. Christmas celebrations today still continue the Virginia traditions of grace and hospitality.

BLESS THIS HOUSE

Oh, thou, who dwellest in so many homes, possess thyself of this. Bless the
life that is sheltered here. Grant that trust and peace and comfort abide within,
and that love and life and usefulness may go out from this home forever.